★★ BASEBALL ★★
SUPERSTARS

RICHARD J. BRENNER

EAST END PUBLISHING, LTD.
Miller Place, New York

Putting It All Together

Roy Halladay has been, by consensus, the best pitcher in baseball during the past decade. Before his rise, however, he suffered a steep fall, starting in 2000, when he slid all the way down, from the Toronto Blue Jays to the low minor leagues.

"I didn't know how to handle failing, and I didn't know how to create confidence," said Halladay, who had been used to dominating hitters since childhood. "When things fell apart, I didn't know how to put them back together."

Fortunately for Halladay, he found help from a pitching coach, who ... with a mechanical issue, and from a ... sports psychologist, who taught him ... how to cope with failure and achieve ... success.

In 2007, his ... back with Toronto, ... 19 games. The ... he notched 2? ... an overwhelming ... winner in the voting for the American League Cy Young Award.

He made a similar transition to the Senior Circuit when he was traded to the Philadelphia Phillies in 2010, winning the National League Cy Young Award that year, while finishing second in the balloting in 2011.

"He's always trying something new to get better," said Phillies pitching coach Rich Dubee. "He's won the Cy Young Award twice, and he's still trying to improve his game."

★ ★ ★ ★ ★

In 2010, Halladay pitched a perfect game, and added a no-hitter in the postseason.

ROY HALLADAY

All in the Family

During his seven seasons as the second baseman for the New York Yankees, Robinson Canó has accumulated a case full of awards. He's won a trio of Silver Slugger Awards as the best-hitting second sacker in the American League, and a Gold Glove for fielding excellence. Canó is also a three-time All-Star and the proud owner of a World Series ring. And on a team that vies for a championship every season, and which has at least three future Hall of Fame candidates on its roster, Canó is generally considered to be the best player now in pinstripes.

"He has the talent to win a batting title, and he's also an incredible fielder with an unbelievable arm," said Larry Bowa, a Major League Baseball Network analyst and a former Yankee coach. "He's turning into a great player. Not a good one, a great one."

But no award or accolade provided Canó with the thrill that he experienced when his father pitched to him in the 2011 Home Run Derby.

🟡 DID YOU KNOW? 🟡

★ ★ ★ ★ ★

Canó was named for Hall of Fame second baseman Jackie Robinson.

"It means a lot to me," said Canó, who, with the help of his father, wound up being crowned the home run king. "He's always been there for me, not just as a dad, but as a friend. I don't want to say that I won the trophy. I want to say that my dad won the trophy."

ROBINSON CANÓ

JACOBY ELLSBURY

The Future is Now

When Pat Casey, the Oregon State baseball coach, watched Jacoby Ellsbury play, it was love at first sight.

"After his freshman year here, I figured that I had a bona fide first round draft pick in my lineup," recalled Casey. "After his second season, I realized that he wasn't going to be just a big leaguer, he was going to be an All-Star. That's how much I believed in his abilities."

The first of Casey's predictions came true when the Boston Red Sox made Ellsbury their first-round pick in the 2005 draft. Two years later, the BoSox promoted the speedy outfielder during a late-season title drive. He rewarded that decision by batting .361, and earning American League Rookie honors for the month of September. Ellsbury continued his hot hitting in the post-season, notching a .360 average, and helping the Red Sox win the World Series.

In 2011, Ellsbury fulfilled the second of Casey's predictions by being picked for the All-Star Game.

DID YOU KNOW?

★ ★ ★ ★ ★

Ellsbury finished second behind Justin Verlander in the 2011 MVP balloting.

But the five-tool centerfielder did more than that; he also won a Silver Slugger Award for his hitting prowess, and a Gold Glove Award for his fielding excellence.

"I don't think he's just becoming a superstar," said teammate David Ortiz. "He's always been a superstar."

JACOBY ELLSBURY

No Comparison Necessary

The first time that Joe Torre, the former Los Angeles Dodgers' manager, saw the 19-year-old Clayton Kershaw pitch, he compared him to another Dodger southpaw hurler, Hall of Famer Sandy Koufax.

"It was about his makeup as much it was about his talent," said Torre. "His I-dare-you-to-hit-me attitude. He had No. 1 written all over him."

Comparisons can create a heavy burden, especially when a teenager is being measured against a three-time Cy Young Award-winner, who is considered by many to be the greatest left-handed pitcher in baseball history. Some people melt under the heat of such high expectations, while others thrive under those white-hot lights.

Four years after Torre's observation, Kershaw took a stride toward justifying the comparison by winning the 2011 National League Cy Young Award. On his way to becoming the youngest pitcher in 27 years to win the award, the 23-year-old captured pitching's Triple Crown by leading the league in ERA and strikeouts and by tying for the lead in wins.

DID YOU KNOW?

★ ★ ★ ★ ★

Kershaw won a Gold Glove in 2011 as the league's best fielding pitcher.

Despite his spectacular 2011 season, Kershaw deflects all comparisons to Koufax, a man whom he greatly admires.

"I'm not trying to be anybody else," said Kershaw. "But I've got expectations for myself that surpass those that anybody else has for me."

CLAYTON KERSHAW

No Comparison Necessary

The sudden emergence of José Bautista as a full-fledged superstar came as a stunning surprise. After six seasons of mediocrity, the Toronto Blue Jays' outfielder finally came into his own, and in 2010, transformed himself into one of the most feared hitters in baseball.

"I had some holes in my swing," said Bautista, who began working with Toronto's hitting coach, Wayne Murphy, at the end of the 2009 season. "I was getting ready too late, and the ball was beating me in the zone. I kept fouling off fastballs and I was too early on breaking balls. I was a more vulnerable hitter, and pitchers took advantage."

DID YOU KNOW?

★ ★ ★ ★ ★

Bautista is a two-time winner of the Hank Aaron Award.

Bautista was the one dishing out the abuse in 2010, however, as he led the majors with 54 home runs and finished among the American League leaders in most offensive categories.

"I knew I had more potential than I'd shown, and that my career numbers hadn't been reflective of the player I could be," said Bautista.

He continued the barrage in 2011, topping the big leagues in homers again, and also setting the pace in walks, on-base percentage, and slugging percentage.

"It's scary," said Terry Francona, the former manager of the Boston Red Sox. "He's become one of the most dangerous hitters in the game. He figured it out at a later stage in his career, but he's figured it out in a *big* way."

JOSÉ BAUTISTA

Doubtless in the Desert

Although Ian Kennedy has had success wherever he has played, scouts have always been skeptical about his ability to achieve at the next level. Those doubts had begun when Kennedy was a schoolboy and they continued even after he'd become a college star and was selected in the 2006 draft by the New York Yankees.

The dark cloud trailing Kennedy was caused by his lack of a big body and a mid-90s fastball, qualities that scouts are trained to value in a pitcher. Those concerns persisted despite Kennedy's excellent performance in the minor leagues. And, in 2008, when he got off to a slow start with the Yankees, even his father began to have doubts.

"I can't say I didn't begin to wonder if he was one of those guys who are great minor leaguers, but not good enough for the big leagues," recalled Sean Kennedy.

But after a trade to the Arizona Diamondbacks, Kennedy bloomed like a desert flower, and in 2011, his second season with the D-backs, he tied for the league lead with 21 wins and emerged as one of the top pitchers in baseball.

DID YOU KNOW?

★ ★ ★ ★ ★

Kennedy finished fourth in the voting for the 2011 Cy Young Award.

"He's very confident," noted Arizona manager Kirk Gibson. "Why shouldn't he be? He's got great stuff."

IAN KENNEDY

The Future is Now

S tarlin Castro, the Chicago Cubs baby-faced superstar, doesn't believe stardom has come his way, and he believes that he'll have to keep improving to...

"I want to keep improving as a ball of player," said Castro, who has been the youngest player in the major leagues for each of his two seasons with the Cubs. "I know I have to work every day to achieve those goals, that's the only way that I can keep getting better."

Castro made an immediate impression in the Windy City by hitting a three-run homer run in his first big league at bat, in 2010. Later in the contest he notched a bases-loaded triple to drive in six RBI. The most ever in a major league debut. He showed that that surge wasn't a fluke by going on to hit .300 as a 20-year-old rookie. Then he really developed in 2011, as he earned selection to the National League All-Star team and led the National League in hits with 207.

★ ★ ★ ★ ★

Castro is the youngest player ever to lead the National League in hits.

"There was a lot of ability and a desire to be the best," said Cubs hitting coach, Rudy Jaramillo. "He has a lot of..."

"It's unbelievable what he's done in such a short time," said Cubs manager Dale Sveum, the 2008 manager of the year. "If he keeps going like this, he's going to be a superstar, no doubt about that."

STARLIN CASTRO

Young and Gifted

How confident were the Minnesota Twins that Joe Mauer, their 20-year-old prospect, was ready to become a big league catcher in 2004? So confident that they traded away an All-Star backstop in order to clear a spot in their lineup for Mauer, despite the fact that he hadn't played a single inning in the majors.

"He has all the skills," said Minnesota manager Rod Gardenhire, explaining the decision. "He does everything effortlessly. You don't see many kids on this stage at his age. It just doesn't happen very often."

Although an injury limited Mauer to only 18 games in 2004, he began to live up to the lofty expectations the following year, when he hit close to .300 and made only five errors.

"He's everything that everyone built him up to be," said former teammate Mike Redmond. "He's got a chance to be a great player in this league for a long time."

Mauer, however, exceeded all expectations by winning three batting titles in four years, while also capturing the 2009 American League MVP Award, and three Gold Glove Awards.

"With what he does behind the plate, controlling the game, and offensively dominating, too, it's amazing," said Twins' first baseman Justin Morneau.

> DID YOU KNOW?
> ★ ★ ★ ★ ★
> Mauer's three batting titles equals the number won by all other catchers.

JOE MAUER

The Dominator

When he was a Little Leaguer, Justin Verlander's fastball was so intimidating that some opposing players refused to bat against him.

Verlander rode his fastball into the Detroit Tigers rotation in 2006, winning 17 games and the American League Rookie of the Year Award. While no opponent skipped an at-bat, none of them relished taking a turn against him.

"Pitchers who can throw as hard as he does have an intimidating edge," said Jeff Kent, the all-time home run hitter among second basemen. "Players don't like to admit it, but it's a fact of life."

Back then, Verlander was, primarily, a flame thrower, who hadn't yet mastered the art of being a pitcher.

"Once he gains a little more experience and develops his secondary pitches to go along with his heater," said former teammate Kenny Rogers, "he's going to become nearly impossible to hit."

> ⚾ **DID YOU KNOW?** ⚾
> ★ ★ ★ ★ ★
> **Verlander pitched the second of his two no-hitters in 2011.**

During the course of the next five seasons, Verlander developed as predicted, and became the most dominating pitcher in the league. He put an exclamation point on his progress in 2011 by leading the league in wins, ERA, and strikeouts. His spectacular season earned him the Cy Young Award, and also allowed him to become the first pitcher since 1992 to capture the MVP Award.

JUSTIN VERLANDER

The Power of Positive Thinking

Millions of boys dream of becoming big league baseball players, but Ryan Braun, the Milwaukee Brewers' leftfielder, had a higher aim.

"My goal wasn't to make it to the big leagues, but to excel once I got there," said Braun. "If you don't strive for greatness in everything you do, you cheat yourself."

Braun took a significant step toward his goal when he won the 2007 Jackie Robinson National League Rookie of the Year Award. He was a hitting machine, posting a .324 batting average, while hammering 34 home runs in only 113 games, and setting the Major League rookie record for slugging percentage with a .634 mark.

"I haven't seen that sort of output from a rookie in my 12 years as a general manager," said Milwaukee G.M., Doug Melvin. "He went well beyond what we anticipated."

During the past four seasons, Braun has made giant strides toward his childhood objective, most notably in 2011, when he helped lead the Brewers to their first division title in 29 years and was named the league's MVP.

DID YOU KNOW?

★ ★ ★ ★ ★

Braun has notched at least 30 homers and 100 RBI for four years running.

"I think I've been a good player, but I believe that I can be a great player," said Braun. "If I didn't have that confidence in myself, I wouldn't be here today."

RYAN BRAUN

JERED WEAVER

The Halo's Dreamweaver

A for posting great strikeout-to-walk numbers as a college junior in 2004, Jered Weaver was the favorite pitcher in that position, ahead of another highly touted pitching prospect, Justin Verlander.

"Weaver is an intense competitor with an excellent feel for his craft, and he can throw strikes with a laser-like precision," raved *Baseball America*.

After the Los Angeles Angels of Anaheim made Weaver their first-round pick, he breezed through their minor league system in a single season. Then he quickly showed that he had big-league stuff by winning his first nine decisions in 2006, tying the American League record for consecutive wins at the start of a career.

Weaver has continued to develop as a pitcher, earning All-Star status the past two seasons, and finishing second behind Justin Verlander in the voting for the 2011 Cy Young Award.

DID YOU KNOW?

★ ★ ★ ★ ★

Weaver pitched and lost against his older brother Jeff, in 2009.

"He can spot his fastball with any pitch, whenever he wants to, and he can change speeds to all his pitches well," marveled the Angels' senior pitching coach Mike Butcher. "He can throw a hard slider, a easy back off, he can throw a slow or hard curveball, change speeds with his fastball and throw a hard or a soft change-up. He's just one step ahead of everybody."

JERED WEAVER

Back to the Future

T he future never looked as bright as the North Star for Josh Hamilton, who was the first overall pick of the 1999 draft. Nicknamed "The Natural," Hamilton seemed to be on a fast track to superstardom.

"It's amazing how many veteran scouts say he's the best player they've ever seen," said Josh Daniels, the general manager of the Texas Rangers.

But Hamilton almost threw away his career and, more importantly, his life and his family, when he became addicted to alcohol and drugs.

"I'm a drug addict," admits Hamilton, whose addictions sidelined him for three seasons. "It's a disease ... ... struggle to any source, and it's going ... to be that way for the rest of my life."

Hamilton ... finally made his big league debut ... in 2007, with the Cincinnati Reds, ... but was traded after the season to the Rangers. He was an instant star in the Texas lineup, and made the first of pair of major appearances in an All-Star team. Hamilton soared even higher in 2010, when he led the Rangers in batting average and in slugging percentage, and was named the American League MVP. His tremendous play also helped lead Texas to the first of two successive World Series appearances.

"I'm proud," says Hamilton, "that I got him to win..."

DID YOU KNOW?

★ ★ ★ ★ ★

Hamilton's all-time favorite player is Cal Ripken, Jr.

JOSH HAMILTON

Bound for Cooperstown

Miguel Cabrera burst into the big leagues in 2003 by banging a walk-off home run in his first major league game. The 20-year-old rookie continued to wield a big bat, and blasted four big flies in the postseason, while helping the Florida Marlins upset the New York Yankees in the World Series.

"He was a natural hitter from the first time I saw him," said Hall of Famer Tony Perez. "Just watch how still he is in the batter's box, and how smooth and compact his swing is. He's as good as it gets."

During his four full seasons with the Fish, Cabrera became the sixth-youngest player to hit 100 home runs, and the third-youngest, after Hall of Famers Ted Williams and Mel Ott, to compile four straight 100 RBI seasons.

After a trade to the Detroit Tigers in 2008, Cabrera adapted quickly to American League pitching, and wound up leading the Junior Circuit in home runs and RBI. And the slugging first baseman seems to keep getting better, as evidenced by his league-leading batting average in 2011.

"He has the talent and the power to be one of the best ever," said Tigers' manager Jim Leyland. "If he keeps playing this way, he's going to end up going straight to Cooperstown."

DID YOU KNOW?

★ ★ ★ ★ ★

Cabrera has averaged more than 100 RBI and 30 homers a season.

MIGUEL CABRERA

Rookie of the Year

No rookie has ever had a greater impact on a season than Buster Posey did in 2010 for the San Francisco Giants. That Posey didn't even play in his first game until the end of May and didn't take over as the starting catcher until July 1 only makes his accomplishments that much more astonishing.

In his first month as the Giants' catcher, Posey went on a 21-game hitting streak, batted .440, and drove in 23 runs for a team that was starving for runs. The 23-year-old backstop was just as impressive behind the plate, handling the Giants' pitching staff and striking fear into would-be base stealers.

"He's Jason Varitek behind the plate and Derek Jeter as a hitter," said Mike Martin, Jr. who coached Posey in college. "He gets inside the ball like Jeter, and he runs the show just like Varitek."

Posey, who was voted the National League Rookie of the Year, continued his high level of play throughout the remainder of the season and the postseason, and he played a pivotal role in powering the Giants to their first World Series win since 1954.

"What Buster did handling the staff, handling himself, and hitting in the heart of the order, shows you what a tremendous kid he is," said Giants manager Bruce Bochy. "It wasn't an easy task we handed him, but he's so mentally strong that nothing we threw at him fazed him."

> ⚾ **DID YOU KNOW?** ⚾
> ★ ★ ★ ★ ★
> Posey was the Giants' first Rookie of the Year since 1975.

BUSTER POSEY

Big-Game Hurler

In the first half of the 2011 season, Chris Carpenter and the St. Louis Cardinals were struggling through the season. After his first eight interactions the ace of the Redbirds' staff was 1-7, and for three 2011 starts of postseason play earned three wins.

"Obviously, I had some bad outings in," some had been," acknowledged Carpenter, a 14-year veteran. "But I wasn't going to give up. I continued to go."

That perseverance was validated in the season's second half, as Carpenter went 10 of 12 decisions, including a couple riding two-hit shutout that allowed the Cards to snatch a playoff spot.

DID YOU KNOW?

★ ★ ★ ★ ★

Chris Carpenter won the National League Cy Young Award in 2005.

Carpenter came up huge again in the... drew up a game of the National League... Division Series when he tossed a... times-hit shutout against Roy... Halladay and the heavily favored... Philadelphia Phillies. Carpenter and the... Cardinals continued their postseason... roll by beating the Milwaukee Brewers in the League Championship Series. They then completed their unlikely run by toppling the Texas Rangers in the World Series, with Carpenter holding the hard-hitting Rangers to two runs over six innings in the Cardinals' Game 7 win.

"Chris Carpenter is the ultimate competitor," said teammate Lance Berkman. "He's the guy we want on the mound in big games."

CHRIS CARPENTER

*This book is dedicated to all people who are courageously, compassionately, and non-violently working to secure universal human rights and attempting to eliminate **all** forms of bigotry and intolerance.*

The book is also dedicated, in loving memory, to my mother and father, Betty and Benjamin Brenner.

My sincere thanks go to Scholastic Book Fairs, for their continued support, and to some of the people who assisted in the creation of this book, including Sarah Becker, Temeka Muse, Elliot Markham, Erin Molta, and James Miceli.

Copy editor: **Erin Molta**   Designer: **James Miceli**

Photo Credits: The cover and interior image of Roy Halladay was photographed by **Christopher Szagola**, and was licensed from Icon Sports Media. Icon also supplied the following images, with the photographer's names in bold: Ian Kennedy, **Chris Pondy**; Starlin Castro, **Warren Wimmer**; Joe Mauer, **Brace Hemmelgarn**; Justin Verlander and Miguel Cabrera, **Steven King**; Ryan Braun and Josh Hamilton, **John Rivera**; Jered Weaver, **John Cordes**. Getty Images supplied the remaining images, as per the following: Robinson Canó, **Nick Laham**; Jacoby Ellsbury, **Jim Rogash**; Clayton Kershaw, **Lisa Blumenfeld**; José Bautista, **Claus Andersen**; Buster Posey, **Ezra Shaw**; and Chris Carpenter, **Dilip Vishwanat**.

ISBN: 0-943403-80-4 * 978-0-943403-80-9

This book was not authorized by Major League Baseball or by any of the players or teams mentioned in this book.

Copyright © 2012 by Richard J. Brenner/East End Publishing, Ltd. All rights reserved. No part of this book may be reproduced or utilized in any form or by any means, electronic or mechanical, including photocopying, recording, or by any information storage and retrieval system, without written permission from the publisher.

Published by EAST END PUBLISHING, LTD.
18 Harbor Beach Road, Miller Place, NY 11764

Printed in the United States of America by Universal Printing Co.

Richard J. Brenner, America's best-selling sportswriter, has written 100 exciting sports titles. To order available titles, email him at: rjbrenner1@gmail.com. Mr. Brenner is also available to speak at schools, libraries, and other venues. For details and fees, you may email him, or write to him c/o East End Publishing.

Author's Message: For many years, Native American groups have been appealing to sports teams not to use logos and names, such as *Braves*, that many people find offensive. Out of respect for, and in support of those appeals, I have chosen not to use such names in this book.